SELF-IMAGE
MASTERY
WORKBOOK

JANINE CONWAY

Self-Image Mastery Workbook by Janine Conway

First Printing: 2019

ISBN-13: 9781794206373

www.JJConway.org

www.HandUpsNotHandOuts.com

JJConway.Teachable.com

JANINE OLIVIA

ENTERPRISES

Also by Janine Conway

(formerly Janine Wiggins)

Focused, Effective, Fundraising

The Trustee Handbook

Overcome Inertia

Fix Your Money, Find Your Honey

Stop Blocking Your Legacy

The 7 Secrets of Abundance Attraction

40 Dates in 4 Months

Healing, My Sisters

Thanks To:

God the Father
My Lord and Savior
The Precious Holy Spirit
And, of course, my loving family!

And also:
Paul Martinelli
Roddy Galbraith
And the ever-encouraging John Maxwell Team

CONTENTS

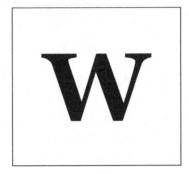

WELCOME

*The most important psychological discovery of
the 20th century is the discovery of the Self Image*

~ Dr Maxwell Maltz

Welcome to Self-Image Mastery. I have been looking forward to this program for a long time! And although am excited about all of our programs in JJ Conway's Empowerment Mentoring Community, I am particularly excited about this one - because it helped me regain confidence after a life-changing accident, and I believe it will be of so much help to so many people, in so many different ways.

This program is a study of happy and successful living through the understanding of the self-image and the role it plays in our lives.

This Self Image Mastery program is packed with great information and rich insights into how to live a truly rich and rewarding life, but it is also intensely practical.

One of the reasons that the discovery of the Self Image is so important is because it is so easy for everyone to understand. Anyone who reads about the Self Image or hears the concepts taught can grasp the significance of the power of the self-concept or Self Image.

And because it is easy to understand, it is easy to implement; you don't need a doctorate in psychology to re-engineer your own Self Image to help you enjoy a more successful life.

DEEP UNTAPPED RESERVOIRS OF TALENT AND ABILITY

Most will readily agree that their mind has far more power and far more potential than they are currently making use of. But if you ask them how to make use of these great untapped reservoirs of talent and ability they have no idea.

The most powerful computer in the universe will do you no good if you don't know how to use its enormous power for your own ends. And if you don't know how to operate the computer, it is useless to you.

Understanding the power of the Self Image gives you a user manual for the mind. A manual that is simple to grasp, easy to understand, and most importantly of all; easy to implement in your life right now, wherever you are at.

YOU CAN DO THIS

As you move through the program, I will not be asking you to do anything that you cannot do. One way to think about the task ahead is this:

You can be successful in life if you can sign your name, remember your address and worry about anything at all!

You have already created a Self-Image and continue to nurture and maintain that Self Image on a daily basis. The good news is that changing it is not really that much more difficult than it was to create in the first place. You will learn to reengineer it in the same way you created it. The only key difference being that you will reengineer it consciously, whereas you created it unconsciously.

DO TODAY'S WORK TODAY

Each chapter of the book represents a week of work within the program. We want you to focus on one part of the process at a time. You will see exercises to complete in advance of each lesson and exercises to complete after each lesson.

Try and set aside some time to complete these exercises if you can. They are not essential for the program to make sense and to be of interest to you, but they are essential for the program to work!

It is extremely important to understand that the Self Image is not changed by collecting information alone but by experiencing. You have to be active. Collecting information is passive whereas experience is active. Positive doing is necessary to change the Self Image, not solely positive thinking.

You will never plough a field by

turning it over in your mind!

There are also exercises in the work book and to test your understanding of the material. It is a good idea to write out your answers in your own words rather than just copying sections out of the workbook or from the lessons. This causes you to process the information at a much deeper level. This significantly enhances not only your recall of the material, but much more importantly, your understanding of the material.

YOUR BEST THINKING GIVES YOU YOUR RESULTS

One final encouragement before we begin this exciting journey together:

Your best thinking has got you where you are today. If you are going to get different, better results in the future, you will need to upgrade your best thinking to <u>better thinking</u>.

In order to do this, you will need to let go of some of your old ideas and cherished opinions and embrace some new ideas. This is typically an uncomfortable process for most people. Don't let this put you off.

Try to avoid the temptation to engage critically with any new ideas that you are not familiar with. They may well be in conflict with some of your existing ideas. If you allow your existing thinking to set about trying to prove that these new ideas won't work, you will be successful, and you will be successful by remaining exactly where you are right now.

You can't actually disprove the ideas in the book and in this program with logic BUT you can **prove** them with experience.

Make up your mind now to practice, experiment and experience this program.

A better question to ask is not 'is this idea right or wrong based on what I know about the world so far? but rather, 'will this idea move me in the direction of my goals?' And if it will, keep an open mind, at least until the end of the program.

Remember that you are wonderfully made, a perfectly imperfect human being, just trying to do your best. Each day remind yourself to be kind to yourself. Allow yourself to trust the process and to enjoy the journey. There is not actually any rush.

Genevieve Behrand said that hurry is fear and is consequently destructive. **A truly successful life is a lifelong love affair with lifelong learning!** Success is not a destination to be quickly and easily achieved so you can put your feet up for the next few decades; success is a way of travelling. You might as well enjoy the journey.

Thank you for allowing me to come alongside you on your journey. I am humbled and honored that you have chosen to join me in this program. I believe it contains some of the best information available for your growth. I certainly hope that you enjoy it and get a great deal from it.

1

AN OVERVIEW OF THE SELF IMAGE
AND AUTOMATIC SUCCESS MECHANISM

It is impossible to outperform your own self image

~ Dr Maxwell Maltz

Dr Harold Bafitis found that when you change a person on the outside, you change their world. The change to how they look on the outside changes how they see themselves on the inside and this changes how they interact with their world, which ends up changing their entire world.

But he also found that sometimes when he changed a person on the outside they continued to have exaggerated ideas of their own ugliness, even after successful surgery.

After decades of successful practice with tens of thousands of patients from all over the world, Dr. Bafitis has found that some people who come for surgery feel like their goals for surgery are met after surgery is complete. But some people do not feel like their goals for surgery are met, even after demonstrably successful surgery. They still FEEL the same as they did before the surgery.

Their original idea that changing the outer appearance of their body will make them feel better is proved to be incorrect. They still feel the same as they did before surgery, even though they look different.

If the image on the outside is changed, but the way the person sees themselves does not, that must mean that the person holds an image of themselves inside that did not necessarily correspond to their appearance on the outside; and that changing how they look on the outside does not necessarily cause a change in how they see themselves on the inside.

If you think this through, it also means that their feelings must somehow stem from the inner image of their appearance rather than their outer image of what they actually look like.

Dr Bafitis has noticed that some people coming for reconstructive or reparative surgery need the surgery. But some people seem to need *spiritual* surgery or *emotional* surgery more than they seem to need *physical* surgery. Some people seem to need all three.

THE SELF IMAGE

Dr Bafitis, like Dr Maltz before him, concluded that this inner image we hold of ourselves is a powerful force in our life. These ideas of the sort of person we are, of how successful we are supposed to be, of how we are meant to think and feel and act in response to our life experiences can be collectively and conceptually labeled as the Self Image.

It is interesting to consider that we are not born with these ideas about ourselves. In fact, we are not born with any ideas at all. Where do these ideas come from then? As you think about this, it quickly becomes obvious that they must come from the experiences of our lives and from our perceptions of those experiences.

Our experiences are stored away as an 'understanding' of the world to help us with future experiences. These personal 'conclusions', or beliefs, often formed unconsciously, are shaped from our positive experiences as well as our negative experiences. Those experiences are sometimes dreadful, sometimes wonderful, sometimes deadly dull!

The more intense the emotions associated with the experience, the more 'important' we unconsciously deem those experiences to be. As a consequence of this, the beliefs are 'filed' with more importance.

Beliefs formed in a moment of terror have a powerful hold over us in the future. Beliefs formed in a moment of joy have a similar power over our future experiences.

Intensely emotional experiences are likely to be more relevant than experiences that are neutral and so this 'ranking' of beliefs is generally useful. Fear charged memories often lead us to avoid similar situations and experiences in the future; joy charged memories often lead us to seek out similar situations and experiences in the future.

These experiences are typically, but not solely, accumulated during the early part of our life and often, not just from our own experiences, but from the comments, actions and responses of other people.

THE SELF IMAGE IS IDEAS ABOUT US, PLACED IN OUR MINDS, BY OTHER PEOPLE, WITHOUT US REALIZING IT, BEFORE WE HAD THE ABILITY TO THINK FOR OURSELVES

Because the beliefs are stored in our subconscious mind, tucked away below the level of consciousness, very often we are not even aware that they are there at all, let alone have cause to question their validity or helpfulness.

Carl Jung observed the impact of this in his famous quote:

UNTIL YOU MAKE THE UNCONSCIOUS CONSCIOUS, IT WILL RULE YOUR LIFE AND YOU WILL CALL IT FATE

From our experiences, we begin to understand our world and we begin to understand other people and most importantly of all, we think we begin to understand ourselves. This understanding of ourselves takes the form of an inner picture or an inner image of what we believe our self to be.

Once these ideas are internalized, as far as we are concerned, they are true. And because we consider them a reflection of reality, there is no point in challenging their validity. After all, what sense does it make to pretend something is other than it is?

These beliefs then drive our behavior, our thinking, our feeling, as well as our perceptions of future experiences and past experiences. Everything that we do is consistent with these beliefs. We act like the sort of person that we believe our self to be. How can we do anything else?

People who believe they are failures, see themselves as failures, they think, feel and act like failures, and it is no surprise that their results then reflect that. Even if they experience some unexpected luck, they find some way to sabotage their own success and snatch failure from the jaws of victory.

People who see themselves as victims find plenty of opportunity every day to be wronged. If they walk around expecting to be offended, guess what they find?

Your self-image is not just the foundation from which your personality emerges, but through your thoughts, feelings and actions, also your circumstances.

YOU CAN CHANGE

The self-image is continually morphing to some degree, and it is critically important to understand and accept that it can be changed. It is not a reflection of reality about you and your potential, rather a reflection of your perception of your past experiences. It is your uneducated guess at your potential, and nothing more.

ARE YOU GOING TO TAKE RESPONSIBILITY?

Your Self Image was largely created without your conscious input or understanding and so, your current Self Image was not your responsibility. It is, however, your responsibility if you want to change it. No one can do that for you. And no one is going to do it for you, even if they could.

Why would you want to change your Self Image? That depends on whether you are experiencing a full life; whether you are happy a good deal of the time; whether you are getting the results you want out of life. It depends on whether you feel like you are living on purpose, making good and sensible use of the talents and abilities you have been given?

If you want to develop and grow and experience more life, you will probably want to work on your Self Image because as Maxwell Maltz said, it is impossible for you to outperform your own Self Image.

If you try to set goals for things you want without changing your Self Image, it will be as Jesus said, like putting new wine into old wine skins. It will be as fruitless as trying to think positively while being thoroughly convinced of negativity.

One of the things that comes close to being THE secret to living more life is to develop a realistic Self-Image; one that you can trust, can associate with, feel proud of and not ashamed of; one that is logical, realistic and helpful to you.

Many, many years before Maxwell Maltz was born, Socrates said, KNOW THYSELF - both your strengths and your weaknesses.

If you have a distorted view of yourself and your Self-Image is one that you are ashamed of, you will tend to shrink away from the world and hide. Your creative expression is then significantly diminished, and you may tend to be angry, resentful and bitter. The more anxiety or fear you feel, the more guilt and shame you may feel, and the more your talents and abilities are extinguished.

But if you are proud of your Self-Image, you will feel confident and step forward into growth, enjoy more happiness and operate far more creatively, freely expressing yourself with confidence and abundance.

In talking about our God given talents and abilities, John Maxwell said,

To give anything less than your best is to sacrifice that gift.

If your Self-Image is stopping you from operating at your best, you are sacrificing your gifts.

The ideas that we hold about our self and our potential, even though they are not accurate, still limit what we can accomplish because they limit what we will try and so they re-define our potential to a massively diminished level. No matter what we are able to do, if we don't do it, we might as well not be able to do it.

THE CREATIVE MECHANISM

Maxwell Maltz identified the way that the Self-Image controls our experience is through the Creative Mechanism. He said that there is within each of us a life force or a life instinct.

Two key elements about the Creative Mechanism that Maltz identified are that it is impersonal and automatic.

Your Creative Mechanism can deliver positive results or negative results, it doesn't mind which, it just delivers what it is told. And it does it automatically. It will act as an automatic failure mechanism or it will act as an automatic success mechanism depending on the goals that you communicate with it. It will deliver goals of happiness and success or goals of misery and failure.

The goals that are acted upon are communicated through images and the most powerful and important of these is the Self Image.

Maltz said that through our experiences, that is through our thoughts and feelings, actions and reactions to what happens to us, we describe the *problem* to be worked upon, the *objective* to be achieved.

If the message that you send your Creative Mechanism most often is that you are not worthy and that you do not deserve to be successful, your Creative Mechanism becomes an Automatic Failure Mechanism.

Your Creative Mechanism uses the 'benefits' of past experiences to assist in solving future problems. It will tap into your vast storehouse of stored information and look for guidance. If you have long memory for every time you've messed up and a very short memory for when you've done well, it will find plenty of evidence to suggest you should steer clear of almost everything!

If you have a long memory for your triumphs and a very short memory for your disasters, it will find plenty of evidence to suggest you plough ahead and make a success of this too.

WHO'S IN CHARGE?

Initially it may be strange to consider that your mind does things that you are not controlling with your attention and your will. But actually, there is far, far more going on with your Spirit and Mind and Body than you are consciously controlling. If you doubt this, 'will yourself' to sweat!

Everyone has had the experience of trying to remember the name of someone, perhaps someone famous. You can see their face in your minds eye but you just can't quite seem to remember what their name is. This scenario brings us face to face with some of these automatic processes.

The more you try and remember (with your will – a conscious faculty) the further the name seems to slip from your grasp. But if you let it go, relax, think of something else, then you allow the image of the person in your minds eye to communicate to your subconscious mind what you need, then in due course it pops unexpectedly into your awareness.

What part of you performed this unconscious search if you did not perform it with your will power?

This simple example illustrates that not only do you not use your will power to communicate with the subconscious mind, but actually, if you try to force it you actually get in the way.

With a little consideration it quickly becomes apparent that there is far more happening on autopilot than we are consciously controlling ourselves.

It becomes obvious that all animals have some kind of built in guidance system that enables them to find food and shelter, to avoid danger and to procreate. Or in other words to survive.

For all animals except one, survival is the goal that their Automatic Success Mechanisms strive to achieve. It is pre-programmed by instinct and they are unable to alter that programming.

But we human beings are different because we have been endowed with Creative Imagination. Using the marvelous power of our marvelous mind we are able to choose any goals we want to lock onto those goals and go after them with everything we've got. No other animal can do this.

It is our imagination that gives us such enormous power to adapt and survive.

Einstein said that imagination is more powerful than knowledge. Henry Ford said that imagination is the workshop of the mind.

Maltz described our brain and our nervous system as a Servo-Mechanism which is in effect an automatic goal striving mechanism.

AUTOPILOT IN A PLANE

The autopilot in a plane accomplishes its goal by moving forward, making mistakes and continually correcting them. It fumbles forward, learning as it goes and eventually zig zags its way to its goal through an endless sequence of mistakes.

Something perhaps worth thinking about: is it possible for you to reach your goals in a similar way?

Most of things that you achieve each day are accomplished with very little conscious will and awareness besides supplying the intention of what you want to achieve.

If you want to move across the room, the intention is sufficient for all of the muscles in our body to fall in line and get you successfully to the other side of the room 'automatically'.

Have you ever watched a baby trying to pick something up when they are very young? The mistakes in movement are large and they typically over-correct with similar clumsy movements. They do not yet have the necessary patterns or habits of movement and motor control to be able to quickly just pick something up without thinking about it.

A baby learns by remembering what works and repeating it in the future, and forgetting all the things that didn't work and not repeating those.

BEFORE THE CALL

Before the live call or before listening to the recording, read the following chapters of Psycho-Cybernetics by Dr Maxwell Maltz:

Preface – The Secret of Using This Book to Change Your Life

Chapter 1 – The Self Image: Your Key to a Better Life

Chapter 2 – Discovering the Success Mechanism within You

If you are unable to read it before joining the call live, that is ok. The calls are stand-alone value. If you do read and contemplate the appropriate chapters in the book, however, you may find that you assimilate the concepts presented and discussed more quickly and more easily.

We are studying the original text: 'Psycho-Cybernetics Deluxe Edition: The Original Text of the Classic Guide to a New Life'

Available from Amazon.com via this link https://amzn.to/2suSNN0 or on Kindle https://amzn.to/2Cqnzvd

AFTER THE CALL

Give some thought to the process questions below and then test your understanding of the material covered so far by answering the reflective questions on the following pages till the end of the chapter.

Where are you now?

Think about what is working for you and what isn't: what is pleasing, what is frustrating... different areas of your life... where can you grow ...where are you doing well... are you doing your best... what's your biggest challenge right now... what's your biggest asset right now etc.

Where are you now continued...

What is your Self Image?

Where did your Self Image come from?

Once formed, how do you think about your Self Image?

How does your Self Image affect your potential?

How does your Self Image affect your potential?

What is the Creative Mechanism?

How do we communicate with the Creative Mechanism?

2

THE STRUCTURE OF THE SELF IMAGE

The development of a realistic Self Image will seem to imbue the individual with new capabilities and new talents

~ Dr Maxwell Maltz

As we move through life, we collect information about ourselves, the world and everyone in it. All of these discoveries are stored away and can be useful in the future.

For example, if you learn that bears tend to try and eat you, this is useful information to help you steer well clear of bears in the future!

If you learn that stone caves tend to have bears in them, this is also useful information that will probably help you stay alive in the future.

At a very young age, information collected is sensory but as we develop and grow and learn a language, we are able to organize the information into more complex, more useful ways. The more we learn, the more sophisticated our information stores might become.

Small bears are not that dangerous and are tasty to eat might be a useful distinction from large black bears are dangerous when with their young; and giant brown bears are always angry and should be avoided at all costs.

Rather than just avoiding all bears, our understanding could develop to the point where we only avoid particular bears at particular times, when advantageous to do so.

The older we get, the more experiences we amass and the amount of information that we have stored continues to grow to an enormous degree.

How do we determine which information is really important and which information is worthless?

If it's true that human beings are largely motivated to seek pleasure and avoid pain, then any information that is associated with pleasure might be valuable information.

Similarly, any information associated with avoiding pain might also be valuable information.

Any information associated with neither pleasurable nor painful experiences might be of very little interest and therefore much less valuable information.

As we saw in the last chapter, emotion then, can be an incredibly useful guide as to what gathered experiences are quickly worth remembering. And in all likelihood, probably the more intense the emotion, the quicker we would want to learn and the more quickly we would want to recall that information in the future.

For example, if bears live in stone caves, we would probably do well to learn that the very first time, from walking into just one stone cave and getting the scare of our life. If we needed the repetition of multiple exposures before we learned, we may well not be around to make use of our learning.

Emotionalized evaluated experiences can be thought of as beliefs. And we form these beliefs about our self, and the world and everyone in it.

All of these beliefs are important, but the beliefs that make up our Self Image are particularly important to our interactions with the world.

Many of the things we believe, we did not originate. Our Self Image is probably made up of our perception of other people's *opinions* of us. And this information was probably internalized by us at an early age, before we could really think for ourselves and decide whether their opinions were valid or just total nonsense.

Our beliefs filter our experience of the world and help us find meaning in life. They also create our emotional world, drive our behavior and end up creating our results.

Where are our beliefs stored?

Because our beliefs are stored in our subconscious minds, they are below our level of awareness and so most of the time, we are not aware of what it is we believe.

Many of the things we believe are poorly, if at all, researched, and if we stopped and thought about it now, we would realize that they don't stand up to scrutiny. The trouble is, most of us never do stop and challenge our beliefs because we confuse them with reality.

As Emerson said,

Of what use to make heroic vows of amendment if the same old lawbreaker is to keep them.

The web of beliefs that make up our Self Image regulate our life in intricate and amazing ways. If we make no attempt to re-evaluate the beliefs that make up our Self Image, any attempts we make at change will likely be frustratingly unfruitful.

We don't need to change everything we believe in order to grow, we may well only need to change or amend a few significant beliefs that are standing in our way, but if we don't become aware of what we believe and challenge the validity of some of those beliefs, we will think that life is happening to us, rather than realizing that we are creating it ourselves.

Self Image re-engineering which we will continually examine through the lessons and exercises of this entire program will help you to analyze and address much of the information internalized in your subconscious.

6 Principles Drawn Out in the Lesson

1. Beliefs are the result of a learning process, not necessarily a reflection of reality

2. We don't start out with beliefs, we acquire them over time

3. Our early learning shapes future learning

4. Beliefs are a strategy for interpreting and finding meaning in life

5. Beliefs demand expression

6. Beliefs can be changed the same way they are formed

AFTER THE CALL

Give some thought to the process questions below and then test your understanding of the material covered so far by answering the reflective questions on the following pages till the end of the chapter.

Following on from last week's question, "Where are you now?" please reflect upon this week's question, **Why are you here?**

Think about all the reasons for your successes and failures.
Where are you stuck... why are you stuck?
Where did you win... why did you when?
Where are you stagnating ... why are you stagnating?
Where you happy ... why are you happy?
Where are you hurting ... why are you hurting?
Where do you have hope ... why do you have hope?
Where do you feel hopeless ... why do you feel hopeless?

There are no right or wrong answers. The questions are designed to challenge you to dig!

Why are you here continued ...

What are beliefs?

What is the root cause of our emotions?

_____

_____

_____

_____

_____

_____

_____

_____

_____

_____

_____

_____

_____

_____

_____

_____

_____

_____

_____

_____

_____

_____

_____

_____

_____

_____

What are the two principle ways that beliefs are formed?

Which beliefs hold the most power over our life experience?

How objective are we in perceiving the world?

What are some of the questions we can use to challenge beliefs?

BEFORE THE NEXT CALL

Before the next live call or before listening to the recording, read the chapter of Psycho-Cybernetics by Dr Maxwell Maltz:

Chapter 3 – Imagination: The First Key to Your Success Mechanism

If you are unable to read it before joining the call live, that is ok. The calls are stand-alone value. If you do read and contemplate the appropriate chapters in the book, however, you may find that you assimilate the concepts presented and discussed more quickly and more easily.

We are studying the original text: 'Psycho-Cybernetics Deluxe Edition: The Original Text of the Classic Guide to a New Life'

Available from Amazon.com via this link https://amzn.to/2suSNN0 or on Kindle https://amzn.to/2Cqnzvd

3

THE POWER OF CREATIVE IMAGINATION

The greatest mistake a man can make is to be afraid of making one

~ Dr Maxwell Maltz

We are different from all of the other animals on the planet. There are many, many similarities between human beings and the other species that exist on earth, but one of the most significant differences is that we have access to the marvelous tool of thought, which gives us the ability to use our imagination creatively.

WE HAVE ACCESS TO CREATIVE IMAGINATION

This means that we can create things in our imagination that do not exist anywhere else in the entire universe. It is our ability to think creatively that gives us infinite potential. There are always better thoughts that we can tap into to enhance anything that has already been created. Nothing is finished.

NOTHING IS DONE PERFECTLY

Everything can be improved. And it will be improved. It is just a matter of time. And it is through the Creative Imagination of human beings that it will be improved.

Despite the incredible power that we have available to us, most people don't make the most of their imaginations. They are always using them, but they are often using them unconsciously, without thinking about what they are creating. They are not using them to improve things, but unwittingly to keep things the same.

Because of this they end up re-creating the same experiences over and over again, rather than using them to create something wonderful, exciting and new.

Imagination gives us great creative ability, but we must learn to use it deliberately and intentionally; we must learn to make the best of it.

Einstein said that

> *Imagination is more powerful than knowledge.*
> *Logic will take you from A to B but*
> *imagination will take you anywhere!*

As creative beings, when we are creating, we tend to be happier than when we are not. A job that allows us no creative expression often feels unexciting, boring and pointless; whereas a job that allows us freedom to create, makes us feel like we are making a difference.

Creative Imagination gives us the ability to create and what better to create than the next best version of ourselves.

We have the ability to use our imagination, not just to imagine what we want to achieve in life, but also who we need to become to achieve it.

WE HAVE THE ABILITY TO CHANGE WHO WE ARE

Changes to the Self Image are made principally through taking action. As Maxwell Maltz says, **positive doing** not just positive thinking.

Because of our marvelous minds, we can use our imagination as a training ground for developing new skills and shaping new attitudes.

We can learn from experience, but not solely physical world experience. By developing our imagination and having the discipline to practice, we can also develop, learn and grow from Mental Movie Experience or what Maxwell Maltz called **Synthetic Experience**.

As we have seen in other chapters, this is because

THE MIND CANNOT TELL THE DIFFERENCE BETWEEN WHAT IS REAL, AND WHAT IS VIVIDLY IMAGINED.

In an extract from an article in Psychology Today:

"... research has revealed that mental practices are almost as effective as true physical practice and that doing both is more effective than either alone."

We can use our marvelous minds to design our life, thinking in advance of all the things we want to achieve.

Then we can use our minds to think about who we need to become or want to become to achieve our goals.

Then we can set about using our minds to start developing the skills, knowledge and experience necessary to become that person.

For someone living a rich, full and rewarding life, these steps are continually iterative.

Notes

Notes

Notes

Notes

AFTER THE CALL

Give some thought to the process questions below and then test your understanding of the material covered so far by answering the reflective questions on the following pages till the end of the chapter.

So far you have looked at **Where are you now**? And then **Why are you here?** This week, give some thought to **What do you want?**

Think about all the things you want: What do you want ... why do you want it ... when do you want it ... think about each different area of your life!

There are no right or wrong answers. The questions are designed to challenge you to dig!

What do you want continued ...

What are the 3 principle sources of images in our mind?

What is Creative Imagination

What is Synthetic Experience?

How many ways can you think of to enhance your creativity?

IMPORTANT: Read this before starting any of the relaxation or visualization exercises.

Only do these exercises when it is safe for you to close your eyes and you have a reasonable chance of not being disturbed for 5 or 10 minutes or so. You can do this exercise standing, sitting or lying down. Perhaps start with sitting upright in a regular chair, feet flat on the floor, hands resting gently in your lap. Experiment with different positions and at different times of the day. Before going to sleep at night can work very well for some people and some exercises.

After waking up in the morning but before getting out of bed is also a great time for some people and some exercises.

It is important to keep in mind that any exercises of this nature can lead to an altered state of consciousness. Although this is quite normal and natural, choose a time when it is appropriate for you to take some time to yourself.

If you have any history of depression do not do any of the exercises in this program without first checking with your doctor. If you are unsure if you should do any of the exercises in this program, make sure you check with your doctor first of all, to reassure yourself it is safe to continue.

Although unlikely, if you experience dizziness or nausea or discomfort of any kind while doing any of these exercises stop immediately by opening your eyes, returning to breathing as normal as soon as you can and contacting your doctor before returning to the exercises.

To begin each exercise, close your eyes gently and just breathe normally for 30 or 40 seconds. When you are ready, take a couple of deep breaths in and out and then return to normal breathing.

You can be aware of the various sounds around you, but try not to control them, try not to judge them, and try not to process them if you can.

You do not need to be perfectly comfortable, perfectly relaxed or in silence to begin. Remember, you do this all the time every day. Everything counts, good enough is good enough.

Visualization Exercise 1 : Observer & Experiencer Part A

This simple exercise is a great way to increase your awareness of how and what you think. It will help you begin to practice the skill of focused attention, develop your ability to quickly relax and it will also help you become more and more aware of your self talk and particularly your inner critic.

If you have not done so before, as you tune in to your own internal chatterbox, you may initially be shocked at how mean you are to yourself! But awareness of how you talk to yourself is the beginning of changing how you talk to yourself, so don't be alarmed, don't be an ostrich ... just stick at it!

If you do, you can eventually become your biggest cheerleader rather than you harshest critic.

Imagine you are staring at a point in the center of your forehead (still with your eyes closed) and just start to gently monitor your thoughts.

You can't do this exercise wrong. If you drift off and completely forget what you are doing, when you realize, bring yourself back to your thoughts and silently comment *how interesting*. Forgive yourself (because this is perfectly normal!) and then continue.

You will probably find the exercise very refreshing and enlightening after just a few minutes.

If you are enjoying the exercise, you can keep going if you like.

When you are done, open your eyes, look around the room, become aware of the sounds around you and think about your experience of observing your own thinking.

- How active was your mind?
- What were you thinking?

- Were you able to control your thoughts?
- How hard to you have to try not to try to control your thoughts?
- What part of you were you able to tap into, to enable you to become the observer of your experience?
- This exercise can be very, very profound.

Practice this exercise once or twice a day until you become very familiar with your thinking.

Visualization Exercise 2 : Mental Movie Experience

This simple exercise builds on the last exercise, so it is best if you have practiced and experimented with the first exercise for several days before you move on.

In this exercise you will become the observer of yourself, but this time as if you were a third party watching you. You will watch this *third party you* perform various activities.

You can design a safe place or a favorite place in your mind which will be the venue for you to watch your movies each time you do this exercise.

You may find it useful to think about the different performances you are going to watch in advance.

You can use this technique to re-watch your past, best experiences. This is an excellent way to feel strong, confident and capable about yourself and your abilities. Very successful people do this naturally. If you do not, you can make a point of doing it deliberately.

You can also use this technique to watch yourself perfectly execute future experiences. You can get experience and familiarity and learning of a future experience in advance! This acts as training for that future experience.

Research has shown that this is almost as good as actual experience. And Mind Movie experience and physical world experience combined are more powerful than either on their own.

Start the exercise in the same way as exercise 1.

Become aware of your thoughts, then imagine yourself sitting in your Mental Movie Venue. Take a moment to notice your surroundings in some detail. What does it look like, feel like, sound like, smell like etc.

Notice where you are sitting. When you are ready and acclimatized, shift your attention to the movie screen. And watch the movie start.

You can use this technique for any aspect of your life but for ease of explanation of the technique, let's imagine you are going to give your first ever after dinner speech in 2 weeks time.

You would work on what you were going to say as normal.

In addition to these sensible preparations, use this technique to become a seasoned speaker!

Watch yourself delivering parts of the speech each day. Notice how you are delivering the speech very, very successfully every time. Notice the details of the delivery.

Make sure the movie is always in the present tense.

Notice the joy on the face of this *you* as they deliver so comfortably and naturally to the audience. Look how eagerly the audience are eating it up. They love it!

As you are creating memories, the details of the information through all relevant senses are important. See the smiles, hear the laughter, feel the sense of accomplishment, smell the food etc.

The more you practice and experiment with this technique, the better you will get at it and the more comfortable and natural it will feel.

BEFORE THE NEXT CALL

Before the next live call or before listening to the recording, read the chapters of Psycho-Cybernetics by Dr Maxwell Maltz:

Chapter 4 – Dehypnotize Yourself from False Beliefs

Chapter 5 – How to Utilize the Power of Rational Thinking

If you are unable to read it before joining the call live, that is ok. The calls are stand-alone value. If you do read and contemplate the appropriate chapters in the book, however, you may find that you assimilate the concepts presented and discussed more quickly and more easily.

We are studying the original text: 'Psycho-Cybernetics Deluxe Edition: The Original Text of the Classic Guide to a New Life'

Available from Amazon.com via this link https://amzn.to/2suSNNo or on Kindle https://amzn.to/2Cqnzvd

4

THE AUTOMATIC FAILURE MECHANISM

Low self-esteem is like driving through life with your handbrake on.

~ Dr Maxwell Maltz

As we go through life, we acquire some bits of information that we assume to be true; information about ourselves, about the world and about everyone in it. Because we assume this information is a true reflection of reality, we don't question its validity. After all, what's the point in that if it is *the way things are*?

Some of this information is very helpful to us. It helps us function in our world and helps us feel positively about things. It leads to us feeling like we are doing well.

Some of this information is very unhelpful to us. It stops us from functioning fully in our world and consequently leads to us feeling like we are not doing well.

The structure of these beliefs in both cases is the same, but the impact on our lives is very, very different.

The rigid hold that our beliefs have over us and our life experience is largely because we assume that they are a reflection of reality. Very often we just experience the effect of this, even if we don't realize that they are there at all.

It is worth mentioning that, even if we do realize we hold certain beliefs, we can still find it difficult to act in defiance of what we *believe*, and this holds true even if we know they are untrue!

For example, someone who struggles with a phobia of flying can read all the statistics in the world about flying being statistically the safest way to travel, but that doesn't stop the images they have in their mind when they think about flying. To them, the feelings are happening; they are very real indeed!

Generally though, we don't realize that we *believe* certain things and these beliefs unconsciously control our perceptions of the world around us. We think we are looking at things the way they are, rather than looking at them just the way we see them.

And the way we see them is through the filter of our beliefs. Our beliefs shape our perceptions, expectations, positions and opinions.

The more we think about this, and reflect upon the power of our beliefs, the more we realize that there is a lot of truth in the statement:

We don't see the world the way it is, we see the world the way we are.

The first time you hear this, it sounds like nonsense. But after thinking about it and reflecting and experiencing the world for some time, the more sense it seems to make.

Ramana Maharshi put it this way:

> ***Don't bother trying to change the world***
> ***because the world you see doesn't even exist.***

If this is true, then changing the world would be as simple as working on your own beliefs!

HOW DO YOU CHANGE YOUR BELIEFS?

A critical first step in taking back control is to understand that we all acquire beliefs and those beliefs are the result of our learning processes. They are not necessarily a reflection of reality.

You have acquired beliefs that are serving you. And you have also acquired beliefs that used to serve you, but that are actually now keeping you stuck where you don't want to be. And you may also have acquired beliefs that have never served you.

Building an image of the person you want to be, in order to have the things you want to have, will bring you up against some of these beliefs. There will existing beliefs that clash with the new ideas that you are now entertaining as you think about the person you want to become; and as you entertain the thinking, feeling and acting that a person like that would engage in.

It can be very illuminating to re-evaluate these old beliefs and examine them in an unemotional, rational way, outside of the context where they normally automatically control your behavior, thinking and feeling.

Sometimes, it very quickly becomes apparent that a belief that you hold, that you have believed for years and years, is completely illogical and actually defies all reason. But because you've never really thought about it, you've never really noticed before just how flimsy its reasoning is.

HOW DO YOU RE-EVALUATE SOME OF THE THINGS YOU BELIEVE?

Here are 3 questions you can ask to expose false beliefs for the fraud that they are:

1.) Is it logical
2.) Is it realistic
3.) Is it helpful

For example, let's say you want to be a public speaker but you believe that you can't be, due to the fact that you are not a natural speaker and so can't bear to speak in front of an audience, because it is just so awful and you always mess up and make a fool of yourself, because you're such an idiot.

Where is the evidence for this belief?

Where is the evidence that there is even such a thing as a natural speaker, let alone that you are not one?

Just because you haven't done something before, does that mean that you can't do it in the future? And can never, ever do it?

Where is the evidence that you can't bear it? If there is any evidence at all, it is probably based on one experience where you didn't do as well as you would like because no one had ever told you how to prepare properly, so you didn't prepare, and you felt uncomfortable. Your ego took a blow because you didn't do it perfectly and you've blown it out of all proportion.

Where is the evidence that you always mess up? Since you always now avoid speaking, all the other instances have probably been imaginary ones in your head which you created!

Where is the evidence that you always make a fool of yourself? Does anyone else even care at all, let alone as much as you do. They are too busy worrying about themselves.

Where is the evidence that this makes you an idiot in all areas of you just because you didn't do as well as you would have liked, one time, in this particular area?

If you get *scientific* about the *facts* that your belief is using against you, you may see that it has frightened you into avoidance and inaction with the sort of *scaremongery* that a child could see through, if it just took the time to look!

INFERIORITY AND SUPERIORITY ARE TWO SIDES OF THE SAME COIN

Maxwell Maltz talks a lot about feelings of inferiority in chapter 4– Dehypnotize Yourself from False Beliefs.

These beliefs of inferiority don't come directly from our experiences but from our perceptions of our experiences.

For example, let's say that you are an average runner and Julia is a very fast runner, you may conclude that Julia is a superior runner than you.

Does that mean Julia is superior to you? Is Julia better than you?

Just because Julia is better than you in one area, does that mean she is better than you in every area?

If you competed in a race with Julia and she beat you by a huge margin, you might conclude that she was the winner and you were a loser.

Does that mean you are a loser in all areas of life?

Because Julia is a faster runner than you, does that mean that you don't measure up, and therefore you are a failure?

Should you feel not worthy? Does that mean that you don't deserve to be happy? You don't deserve Success?

If you feel bad when you lose to Julia, do you feel good when you beat Alex?

If you hadn't raced Julia and only Alex, would that mean that you are superior to Alex? Does it mean Alex is a loser? Would you then feel like a winner?

It's amazing how we can blow things out of all proportion and end up thinking and believing that things mean what we expected them to mean, even when they don't!

The obvious truth is that you are neither better than Alex or inferior to Julia. You are you.

You are worthy.

If you see yourself as better than other people, you will also see yourself as inferior to other people at times.

If you buy into the *comparison game*, you are setting yourself up to be disappointed and emotionally disturbed.

What happens as you grow older and weaker and slower? How will you ever be happy again? How will you ever feel like a winner as you age if your self-worth is dependent on being the fastest, or the biggest or the strongest or the prettiest?

There will always be someone faster, coming around the corner.

Dennis Waitly put it very well:

You are as good as the best but no better than the rest

The standards that you judge yourself by and judge others by may very well not even be your standards anyway. They could be the standards of other people from your childhood that you have accepted unquestioningly.

Really thinking about what YOU think, independently of the influences of other people in your environment and independently of the influences of your conditioned mind can be very liberating.

A good way to approach this is to focus on what comes up when you move forward in pursuit of your goals.

Notes

Notes

Notes

Notes

Notes

Notes

Notes

AFTER THE CALL

Give some thought to the process questions below and then test your understanding of the material covered so far by answering the reflective questions on the following pages till the end of the chapter.

So far you have looked at **Where are you now**? And then **Why are you here?** And **What do you want?** Now think about **Who do you need to become** to have it?

Think about the people you know who have the life you want in each area: what are they like? How do they think? How do they behave? What do they do? What do they *not* do? What will they stand for? What will they *not* stand for? Think about this for each of the different areas you identified in the *What do You Want* exercise.

There are no right or wrong answers. The questions are designed to challenge you to dig!

Who do you need to become continued ...

Who do you need to become continued ...

IMPORTANT: Read this before starting any of the relaxation or visualization exercises.

Only do these exercises when it is safe for you to close your eyes and you have a reasonable chance of not being disturbed for 5 or 10 minutes or so. You can do this exercise standing, sitting or lying down. Perhaps start with sitting upright in a regular chair, feet flat on the floor, hands resting gently in your lap. Experiment with different positions and at different times of the day. Before going to sleep at night can work very well for some people and some exercises.

After waking up in the morning but before getting out of bed is also a great time for some people and some exercises.

It is important to keep in mind that any exercises of this nature can lead to an altered state of consciousness. Although this is quite normal and natural, choose a time when it is appropriate for you to take some time to yourself.

If you have any history of depression do not do any of the exercises in this program without first checking with your doctor. If you are unsure if you should do any of the exercises in this program, make sure you check with your doctor first of all, to reassure yourself it is safe to continue.

Although unlikely, if you experience dizziness or nausea or discomfort of any kind while doing any of these exercises stop immediately by opening your eyes, returning to breathing as normal as soon as you can and contacting your doctor before returning to the exercises.

To begin each exercise, close your eyes gently and just breathe normally for 30 or 40 seconds. When you are ready, take a couple of deep breaths in and out and then return to normal breathing.

You can be aware of the various sounds around you, but try not to control them, try not to judge them, and try not to process them at all if you can avoid it.

You do not need to be perfectly comfortable, perfectly relaxed or in perfect silence to begin.

Remember, you do this all the time, every day. Everything counts, good enough is good enough.

Visualization Exercise 3 : Observer & Experiencer Part B

In this version of the Observer & Experiencer exercise, you will start in exactly the same way as you have done in Part A.

This simple exercise is a great way to increase your awareness of how and what you think. It will help you begin to practice the skill of focused attention, develop your ability to quickly relax and it will also help you become more and more aware of your self talk and particularly your inner critic.

If you have not done so before, as you tune in to your own internal chatterbox, you may initially be shocked at how mean you are to yourself! But awareness of how you talk to yourself is the beginning of changing how you talk to yourself, so don't be alarmed, don't be an ostrich ... just stick at it!

If you do stick at it, you can eventually become your biggest cheerleader rather than you harshest critic.

Imagine you are staring at a point in the center of your forehead (still with your eyes closed) and just start to gently monitor your thoughts.

You can't do this exercise wrong. If you drift off and completely forget what you are doing, when you realize, bring yourself back to your thoughts and silently comment *how interesting*. Forgive yourself (because this is perfectly normal!) and then continue.

You will probably find the exercise very refreshing and enlightening after just a few minutes.

If you are enjoying the exercise, you can keep going if you like.

In the second part of this version of the exercise, you will flip from the observer of your thinking and feeling to the experiencer.

Rather than mentally stepping outside yourself to witness what is going on as a 3rd party might, now try mentally stepping backside to experience what is going on as you.

After several minutes of practice, trying switching between the two. Become the observer of your experience for a period of time; then switch to being the experiencer of it.

Be a 3rd party observing from the outside for a period of time then switch to being you experiencing from the inside.

Don't be attached to any particular outcome other than practicing and experimenting. You may have an automatic tendency to berate yourself for not doing it right! Catch yourself as early as you can if this happens, switch to the observer and witness how you talk to yourself.

The next time it happens and you catch it, stay in the experience of how you talk to yourself.

Most people struggle with these types of exercise. You cannot do this exercise wrong.

Just practice, experiment and experience!

When you are done, open your eyes, look around the room, become aware of the sounds around you and think about your experience of observing and experiencing your own thinking.

- How active was your mind?
- What were you thinking?
- Were you able to control your thoughts?
- How hard to you have to try not to try to control your thoughts?
- What part of you were you able to tap into, to enable you to become the observer of your experience?
- This exercise can be very, very profound.

Practice this exercise once or twice a day until you become very familiar with your thinking.

As you enjoy this exercise more and more, spend longer each time in the exercise.

Visualization Exercise 4 : Rehearsal Experience

This exercise builds on Visualization Exercise 3, so it is best if you have practiced and experimented with this one for several days, and ideally exercises 1 & 2 as well, before you move on to this exercise.

In this exercise you will become the **experiencer** of yourself performing various activities.

In exercise 2 you watched movies of yourself in a certain venue. In this exercise you will experience yourself performing in *real life*. So the setting will be wherever the experience would normally take place. If you are rehearsing on stage at a key customers' offices, then that's what you will imagine.

At first, you may find it useful to think about the different roles you are going to perform in advance.

The key difference between exercise 2 and this exercise is even though you may use the same scenario, the exercises are different. In exercise 2 you are watching you perform as if you were a 3rd party looking on. And in this exercise, you are experiencing it through your own eyes and ears.

Using both exercises is a great way to to feel strong, confident and capable about yourself and your abilities. Very successful people do both of these exercises very naturally. If you do not, you can make a point of doing it deliberately.

Research has shown that this is almost as good as actual experience. And Mind Movie Experience, Rehearsal Experience and physical world experience, altogether are more powerful than either on their own.

When you are ready to start the exercise, start in the same way as the other exercises.

Become aware of your thoughts, then imagine yourself in the setting where you want to perform perfectly.

Take a moment to notice your surroundings in some detail. Where are you? What does it look like, feel like, sound like, smell like?

Be there, in the moment.

You can use this technique for any aspect of your life but for ease of explanation of the technique, let's imagine you want to be more comfortable in conversation with your customers.

It would make perfect sense for you to work on what you were going to say and to do all your research and homework as normal.

In addition to these sensible preparations, use this technique to become more natural and relaxed when with your customers.

Relive some of your best ever sales conversations. What does it feel like? Remember this is present tense – it is happening now. Experience and enjoy it.

Create some new performances and experience them as if you where remembering them. But once again, relive them in the present tense.

Make sure you are always experiencing in the present tense.

Look out at the joy on the face of your customers, feel the warmth and strength of character in the handshake of your client; notice how you perform every detail perfectly. Notice how good it feels to see your customers enjoying the conversation and enjoying placing orders for more services. Notice how good it feels. How relaxed you are. Notice how much you are enjoying it and how much they are enjoying it also.

As you are creating memories, the details of the information through all relevant senses are important. See the smiles, hear the laughter, feel the sense of accomplishment, smell the food etc.

The more you practice and experiment with this technique, the better you will get at it and the more comfortable and natural it will feel.

Activity Exercise 5 : Doing New Things

This is the simplest exercise to do but do not let its simplicity fool you! This exercise is very enlightening; very insightful; very enabling. But only if you actually do it.

Changes to your results will come from changing your self-image. Changing your self image will come largely from positive action – from doing different things.

You are in the habit of doing the same things. You need to consciously go against these habits.

A simple way to do this is to do something different every day. On the first day it could be as simple as driving a different route. As you experiment, however, try and vary many different aspects of life. If you always respond in a certain way to certain questions, challenge yourself to respond in different ways.

The exercise is not to become aware of how automatic daily life is and how those daily actions produce your current results. Changing your actions can lead to different results. It can also lead to changes to the self image.

Try and be creative as you can. Keeping a log of the things you are trying differently will help greatly.

BEFORE THE NEXT CALL

Before the next live call or before listening to the recording, read the chapters of Psycho-Cybernetics by Dr Maxwell Maltz:

Chapter 6 – Relax and Let Your Success Mechanism Work for You

If you are unable to read it before joining the call live, that is ok. The calls are stand-alone value. If you do read and contemplate the appropriate chapters in the book, however, you may find that you assimilate the concepts presented and discussed more quickly and more easily.

We are studying the original text: 'Psycho-Cybernetics Deluxe Edition: The Original Text of the Classic Guide to a New Life'

Available from Amazon.com via this link https://amzn.to/2suSNN0 or on Kindle https://amzn.to/2Cqnzvd

5

STRESS AND RELAXATION

*Successful people are able to rise above crises
by relaxing no matter what the external situation*

~ Dr Maxwell Maltz

The human body is a wonderful thing. There is so much going on in every single second within your body, that it is difficult to comprehend the enormity of what is happening.

According to the latest estimates, your body is made up of around 35 trillion cells!

If you try to calculate the total number of chemical reactions, every second, for all of these cells, the number is so huge, it is difficult to even comprehend.

All of this goes on without your conscious involvement or conscious awareness.

If you are like most people, even with some of the better-known activities like digesting a meal, you are probably clueless as to how it actually works, and you certainly have no conscious role in it, even if you do understand the ins and outs of digestion.

Your body is marvelous indeed.

When it comes to the experience of stress and particularly your body's response to stress, there is also a lot going on that you probably don't understand and probably don't have any conscious involvement in.

The same is almost certainly true of your body's process of relaxation.

Understanding what happens in that marvelous body of yours when you are faced with stressful situations can help you get better at dealing with stress, and it can also help you learn how to relax.

Learning how your body relaxes can help you get better at relaxing and help you relax much more deeply, much more quickly. And a combination of understanding the physiology of stress and the physiology of relaxation, coupled with the regular practice of relaxation techniques and exercises can really equip you to deal with the constant challenges of 21st century life.

THE AUTONOMIC NERVOUS SYSTEM

The part of your nervous system that you are unable to control with your will power is called the autonomous nervous system. There are two key parts or pathways to the autonomous nervous system:

1. The Sympathetic Pathway
2. The Parasympathetic Pathway

Both these parts of the nervous system are continually working and work antagonistically with one another. It may be helpful to think of the **sympathetic** pathway as the **fight or flight** pathway and the **parasympathetic** pathway as the **rest and digest** pathway.

As suggested by the fight or flight label, the sympathetic nervous system is mainly activated by stress. It then prepares the body to fight or to flee. This is a basic survival mechanism. When it is activated there are certain changes in the body:

- Heart rate increases
- Blood pressure goes up
- Blood sugar increases
- Pupils dilate
- And many others

From a survival perspective, it is important that all these things happen very rapidly and automatically.

The parasympathetic nervous system, when activated, has the opposite effect on the body to the sympathetic nervous system – it has a calming effect:

- Lowers heart rate
- Lowers blood pressure
- Promotes digestion
- And many others

When you breathe in and out you activate the autonomic nervous system. Breathing in tends to activate the sympathetic nervous system a little bit. And breathing out tends to activate the parasympathetic nervous system a little bit. This is why most meditation systems and relaxation systems focus on a prolonged outbreath.

The outbreath is the relaxation breath

Understanding the physiology of stress and relaxation is very useful as a starting point, but it is essential to practice relaxation to get proficient at it and to reach the point where you are able to quickly and easily relax your body by eliciting the relaxation response.

The exercises in this workbook are designed to help you get more and more effective at eliciting the relaxation response. But they only work if you actually do them, and do them regularly.

Notes

Notes

Notes

Notes

Notes

Notes

Notes

AFTER THE CALL

Continue to give thought to the two key future questions:

- What do you want?
- Who do you need to become to have it?

You will probably want to keep coming back to these two questions as you continue to formulate your ideas and gain clarity on what your ideal life looks like.

As you gain clarity on how you want to live your life, write out in each area of your life, **what does success look like for the successful person you want to be?**

It may help you to think about it for each of the following questions, for each of the five key areas of your life (and any others you want to include):

- **What success are you enjoying?**
- **What are you doing?**
- **What skills have you mastered?**
- **Where are you using them?**
- **How are you thinking?**
- **How are you feeling?**
- **How are you acting?**
- **How are you reacting?**
- **How are you interacting with other people?**
- **How do they see you?**

In the area of **Spiritual Growth**:

In the area of **Key Loving Relationships**:

In the area of **Physical Health**:

In the area of **Your Chosen Vocation**:

In the area of **Financial Health**:

In Any **Other Areas** you choose:

IMPORTANT: Read this before starting any of the relaxation or visualization exercises.

Only do these exercises when it is safe for you to close your eyes and you have a reasonable chance of not being disturbed for 5 or 10 minutes or so. You can do this exercise standing, sitting or lying down. Perhaps start with sitting upright in a regular chair, feet flat on the floor, hands resting gently in your lap. Experiment with different positions and at different times of the day. Before going to sleep at night can work very well for some people and some exercises.

After waking up in the morning but before getting out of bed is also a great time for some people and some exercises.

It is important to keep in mind that any exercises of this nature can lead to an altered state of consciousness. Although this is quite normal and natural, choose a time when it is appropriate for you to take some time to yourself.

If you have any history of depression do not do any of the exercises in this program without first checking with your doctor. If you are unsure if you should do any of the exercises in this program, make sure you check with your doctor first of all, to reassure yourself it is safe to continue.

Although unlikely, if you experience dizziness or nausea or discomfort of any kind while doing any of these exercises stop immediately by opening your eyes, returning to breathing as normal as soon as you can and contacting your doctor before returning to the exercises.

To begin each exercise, close your eyes gently and just breathe normally for 30 or 40 seconds. When you are ready, take a couple of deep breaths in and out and then return to normal breathing.

You can be aware of the various sounds around you, but try not to control them, try not to judge them, and try not to process them at all if you can avoid it.

You do not need to be perfectly comfortable, perfectly relaxed or in perfect silence to begin.

Remember, you do this all the time, every day. Everything counts, good enough is good enough.

Visualization Exercise 2 & 4 : Mental Movie Experience and Rehearsal Experience

Continue to experiment and practice with the visualization exercises you have been doing for the last two weeks. If you have a favorite, then it is ok to do more of that one.

As you get clear on the person you will become, include that in your visualization exercises. See yourself, feel yourself, experience yourself as that person with the details you are getting clearer on from this week's process exercises.

You will probably continue to shape some of these details for some time – all the while getting clearer and clearer about who you need to become to live the way you want to live.

As you get clearer, keep visualizing with those details and experiences.

As before, remember, you are creating memories, the details of the information through all relevant senses are important. See the smiles, hear the laughter, feel the sense of accomplishment, smell the food etc.

The more you practice and experiment with these techniques, the better you will get at it and the more comfortable and natural it will feel.

Activity Exercise 5 : Doing New Things

Continue with this exercise and become more and more aware of how habitual you are in every area of your life.

Be as creative as you can with new ways you can respond to life.

Relaxation Exercise 6 : Humming Breathing Relaxation Exercise

This is a very simple exercise. Make sure you have read the section on page 117 entitled:

IMPORTANT: Read this before starting any of the relaxation or visualization exercises.

Find somewhere quiet to sit or lie down.

Close your eyes gently and breath normally for a moment or two.

When you are ready switch to breathing through your nose if you are not already. Make sure you are reasonably comfortable breathing through your nose. You may have a slight blocked nose, but if it is clear enough to breath, you may find it quickly unblocks as you do this exercise.

If you are unable to breath in through your nose, try breathing in through your mouth at first and then try periodically to breath in through your nose during the exercise.

Breath in quite deeply to a rough count of around five.

Them hum as you breath out. Try to keep the exhalation going for longer than the inhalation. As you are humming you should easily be able to manage this.

The longer the exhalation, as long as you are comfortable, the better.

When you have exhaled all the way out and you are ready for another round, repeat with an in breath.

After a few minutes of this, open your eyes and make sure you are comfortable. Then continue if you like.

After experimenting for a few sessions, your goal is to breath in deeply and hum all the way out for as long as you are enjoying it.

When you have grown tired of humming, simply return to normal breathing and relax, nap or get up.

IF YOU FEEL ANY DISCOMFORT OR DIFFICULTY BREATHING AT ANY TIME, OPEN YOUR EYES AND RETURN TO NORMAL BREATHING AS SOON AS YOU CAN.

BEFORE THE NEXT CALL

Before the next live call or before listening to the recording, read the chapters of Psycho-Cybernetics by Dr Maxwell Maltz:

Chapter 7 – You Can Acquire the Habit of Happiness

Chapter 8 – Ingredients of the Success Type Personality and How to Acquire Them

If you are unable to read it before joining the call live, that is ok. The calls are stand-alone value. If you do read and contemplate the appropriate chapters in the book, however, you may find that you assimilate the concepts presented and discussed more quickly and more easily.

We are studying the original text: 'Psycho-Cybernetics Deluxe Edition: The Original Text of the Classic Guide to a New Life'

Available from Amazon.com via this link https://amzn.to/2suSNN0 or on Kindle https://amzn.to/2Cqnzvd

6

THE HABIT OF HAPPINESS

Happiness is simply a state of mind in which our thinking is pleasant a good share of the time.

~ Dr Maxwell Maltz

Maxwell Maltz states in the book that happiness is simply a state of mind in which our thinking is pleasant a good share of the time. Not all the time, but a good share of the time. And not in a continual state of ecstasy or bliss but a state in which our thinking is *pleasant*.

No one is one hundred percent happy one hundred percent of the time. No one is *completely* happy.

Just like no one is one hundred percent good all the time. No one is completely good.

And no one is one hundred percent bad all the time. No one is completely bad. Everyone is a bit of a mix.

No one is perfect. Everyone is perfectly imperfect and that's the way it's supposed to be.

So it's probably a reasonably accurate statement to say, everyone wants to be happier. And everyone probably wants to be healthier and wealthier too!

Happiness (and health and wealth) is not something that can be sought directly. Happiness, health and wealth are very similar to success in this regard.

Napoleon Hill said:

Success is the progressive realization of a worthy ideal.

Success then is the result of pursuing meaningful goals and making some progress towards them.

Happiness also comes as a biproduct of your activities in specific areas that are of value to you.

THE HABIT OF HAPPINESS

As we have discussed in previous chapters, human beings are creative beings. Your power of intention, through your imagination, gives you the extraordinary ability to create.

Intention gives us great power. It is a good idea to set the general intention that you want to be happy. This conscious use of your intention will not automatically make you happier (as we've already seen, happiness is not something that can be sought directly) but it will certainly help to displace the unconscious use of your intention to make yourself unhappy.

THE HABIT OF HAPPINESS

By consciously setting the intention to be happy, you are stating that being happy is important to you and that you are going to make time for it.

There are a number of different things you can do to try and keep your focus on what is good about your life, rather than what is bad.

Things like:

- Simplifying your life
- Prioritizing what is important to you
- Making efforts every day to live on purpose
- Remembering to be grateful for what you have
- Remembering to grateful for who you are

Perhaps the best habit to get into, is the habit of serving others. When you take youR attention off of yourself and place it deliberately onto how you can help others, something magical happens.

Albert Schweitzer put this best:

Only those of you who find a way to serve your fellow man will ever really be truly happy

One of the best ways to *find* happiness is to look for ways that you are able to use your God given talents and abilities in the service of others, so that you can develop and grow in your area of giftedness, whilst at the same time helping your fellow man.

If you don't know what your area of giftedness is, follow your interests. Most people don't know *what they want to be when they grow up*, they have to find out. Experiencing life is how you find out.

Notes

Notes

Notes

Notes

Notes

Notes

Notes

AFTER THE CALL

This program is about becoming. Continue to give thought to the two key future questions:

- What do you want?
- Who do you need to become to have it?

You will probably want to keep coming back to these two questions as you continue to formulate your ideas and gain clarity on what your ideal life looks like.

Continue to write out in each area of your life, **what does success look like for the successful person you want to be?**

Most people can't do this in one go. The more time you spend on it, the better will be the end result.

You will find that as you think about it for a period of time, and then forget about it for a period of time, during the periods when you are just letting it sit in your subconscious, you get all sorts of ideas that you will want to include in your image of success, happiness, wealth and wellness.

Try and develop as many *Success Scenes* as you can for each of the key areas of your life. Play them on your Mental Movie Experience screen and experience them in Rehearsal Experience. Stick to present tense, happening *now* and use perfect performance where you are enjoying the success you want in your life. You are that person in your Mental Training.

Remember you are creating memories!

As you develop more and more Success Scenes for each area, pick one for each that is representative of your success in that area. Write this Success Scene out in multi-sensory detail in the following sections.

Key Success Scene in the area of **Spiritual Growth**:

Key Success Scene in the area of **Key Loving Relationships**:

Key Success Scene in the area of **Physical Health**:

Key Success Scene in the area of **Your Chosen Vocation**:

Key Success Scene in the area of **Financial Health**:

Key Success Scene in the area of **Other Areas** you choose:

IMPORTANT: Read this before starting any of the relaxation or visualization exercises.

Only do these exercises when it is safe for you to close your eyes and you have a reasonable chance of not being disturbed for 5 or 10 minutes or so. You can do this exercise standing, sitting or lying down. Perhaps start with sitting upright in a regular chair, feet flat on the floor, hands resting gently in your lap. Experiment with different positions and at different times of the day. Before going to sleep at night can work very well for some people and some exercises.

After waking up in the morning but before getting out of bed is also a great time for some people and some exercises.

It is important to keep in mind that any exercises of this nature can lead to an altered state of consciousness. Although this is quite normal and natural, choose a time when it is appropriate for you to take some time to yourself.

If you have any history of depression do not do any of the exercises in this program without first checking with your doctor. If you are unsure if you should do any of the exercises in this program, make sure you check with your doctor first of all, to reassure yourself it is safe to continue.

Although unlikely, if you experience dizziness or nausea or discomfort of any kind while doing any of these exercises stop immediately by opening your eyes, returning to breathing as normal as soon as you can and contacting your doctor before returning to the exercises.

To begin each exercise, close your eyes gently and just breathe normally for 30 or 40 seconds. When you are ready, take a couple of deep breaths in and out and then return to normal breathing.

You can be aware of the various sounds around you, but try not to control them, try not to judge them, and try not to process them at all if you can avoid it.

You do not need to be perfectly comfortable, perfectly relaxed or in perfect silence to begin.

Remember, you do this all the time, every day. Everything counts, good enough is good enough.

Visualization Exercise 2 & 4 : Mental Movie Experience and Rehearsal Experience

Continue to experiment and practice with the visualization exercises you have been doing for the last few weeks. If you have a favorite, then it is ok to do more of that one.

As you get clearer and clearer on the person you will become, include that in your visualization exercises.

See yourself, feel yourself, experience yourself as that person with the details you are getting clearer on from this week's process exercises.

You will probably continue to shape some of these details for some time – all the while getting clearer and clearer about who you need to become to live the way you want to live.

As you get clearer, keep visualizing with those details and experiences.

As before, remember, you are creating memories, the details of the information through all relevant senses are important. See the smiles, hear the laughter, feel the sense of accomplishment, smell the food etc.

The more you practice and experiment with these techniques, the better you will get at it and the more comfortable and natural it will feel.

Activity Exercise 5 : Doing New Things

Continue with this exercise and become more and more aware of how habitual you are in every area of your life.

Be as creative as you can with new ways you can respond to life.

- Are you thinking in new ways?
- Are you acting in new ways?
- Are you able to generate different feelings to normal in the same situations?
- Are you able to deliberately perceive things in different ways?
- Are you able to believe something different than normal?
- Are you able to be very deliberate when you would normally be on autopilot?
- Are you able to be kind when you would normally be critical?
- Are you able to be optimistic when you would normally be cynical and pessimistic?

Relaxation Exercise 7 : Progressive Body Relaxation

This is a very simple exercise. Make sure you have read the section on page 117 entitled:

IMPORTANT: Read this before starting any of the relaxation or visualization exercises.

Find somewhere quiet to sit or lie down. This exercise can be done almost anywhere in almost any position, even standing up, but it is a lot easier and a lot more enjoyable to do lying down.

Close your eyes gently and breath normally for a moment or two.

If you enjoyed the previous exercise with humming, start out with 2 or 3 minutes of this to begin relaxing.

When you are ready, simply return to normal breathing and continue to relax.

You can choose whether you start at your toes and fill your body up with relaxation; or start at the top of your head and allow the relaxation to spill down through your body all the way to your toes. Experiment with both approaches and see which you prefer.

Using your conscious attention and focus, simply move through your body, placing your attention on each specific part of your body and *breathe into* that body part. As you breathe for a moment or two, allow that body part to relax. You will probably be surprised by how much unconscious tension there is in your muscles.

Blood flow is amenable to suggestion and so as you focus and breath your body relaxes more and more.

Use the same anchor that you used for the breathing exercise. Your right or left (be consistent) hand on your abdomen works well.

When you have gone through your entire body, simply enjoy the wonderful feeling of relaxation.

Sometimes you may want to spend some time on your Success Scenes.

Sometimes you may just want to enjoy allowing your body the time to rest and renew.

Sometimes you may just want to enjoy a refreshing nap.

Or I could be your entrance into a good night's sleep.

If you need to wake up after a certain time, set an alarm. You will proably wake up on cue, but just in case, set an alarm as far out as possible so you don't create a feeling of rushing.

If you are not going to sleep for the night when you've finished, simply wake up and get up slowly in your own time.

You may find it a good habit to get into, to think of a few things that you are grateful for before you continue with your life!

IF YOU FEEL ANY DISCOMFORT OR DIFFICULTY BREATHING AT ANY TIME, OPEN YOUR EYES AND RETURN TO NORMAL BREATHING AS SOON AS YOU CAN.

BEFORE THE NEXT CALL

Before the next live call or before listening to the recording, read the chapters of Psycho-Cybernetics by Dr Maxwell Maltz:

Chapter 8 – Ingredients of the Success Type Personality and How to Acquire Them

Chapter 11 – How to Unlock Your Real Personality

If you are unable to read it before joining the call live, that is ok. The calls are stand-alone value. If you do read and contemplate the appropriate chapters in the book, however, you may find that you assimilate the concepts presented and discussed more quickly and more easily.

We are studying the original text: 'Psycho-Cybernetics Deluxe Edition: The Original Text of the Classic Guide to a New Life'

Available from Amazon.com via this link https://amzn.to/2suSNN0 or on Kindle https://amzn.to/2Cqnzvd

PROGRAM SUMMARY

The secret of change is to focus all of your energy,
not on fighting the old, but on building the new.

~ Socrates

Personal Growth is so important in life. Most people struggle with one area of life or another, almost all the time. Everyone needs help, although most people do not like to admit it. As John Maxwell said,

The only guarantee that tomorrow will be better, is if you are growing today.

Personal growth is the answer to life's challenges and struggles. But personal growth takes time, energy and effort.

Personal growth is never convenient, it is seldom comfortable and always frustrating. The choice to grow, therefore, needs to be taken again and again and again.

In preparation for the final call, think about some of the areas that you have already grown throughout this program. Think about areas of transformation and breakthrough that you can share to inspire other people in the program.

Think about challenges you are already thinking about as you move on to continuing your personal growth without the energy of support of this community. It is so easy to slip back into the old, familiar, comfortable way of doing things. This is the default option that we have to avoid against every single day.

John Maxwell said,

Everything worthwhile is uphill.

This means the decision to grow is a decision to climb, because your worthy ideals are always going to be uphill. Growth is always uphill. Climbing up hill is never something that happens by default. Sliding downhill is what happens by default. Climbing up hill always has to be intentional.

As we conclude this program, make a conscious commitment that you will continue your journey of personal growth. Look for books, products and programs that are congruent with your journey. Look for communities of like-minded people to encourage you as you grow. You can easily find products, programs, and like-minded people at JJConway.Teachable.com.

Thank you for joining us in this program. The program has been better because you chose to be a part of it. We are grateful that you did. Keep your eye on the prize, personal growth will get you there, it is worth it in the end, and always remember, your growth is always yours to keep.

Good luck on your journey and may God bless your valiant and noble efforts to grow. The world needs a better you. You can do no more than do your best. And your best is all it takes!

A truly successful life is a lifelong love affair with lifelong learning

Notes

Notes

Notes

Appendix

The self-image is changed, for better or worse, not by intellect alone, nor by intellectual knowledge alone, but by "experiencing." Wittingly or unwittingly you developed your self-image by your creative experiencing in the past. You can change it by the same method.

~ Dr Maxwell Maltz

This part of the workbook contains several exercises from the live class that will help you uplevel your self-image. In effect, you will be crafting the life you desire to live – first in the imagination, and then, as you hold that image at the forefront of your life, in the physical realm.

If you aren't already a part of our online course, please visit JJConway.teachable.com to register for one of personal growth courses.

My Success Timeline: Proof that I can be successful in some areas

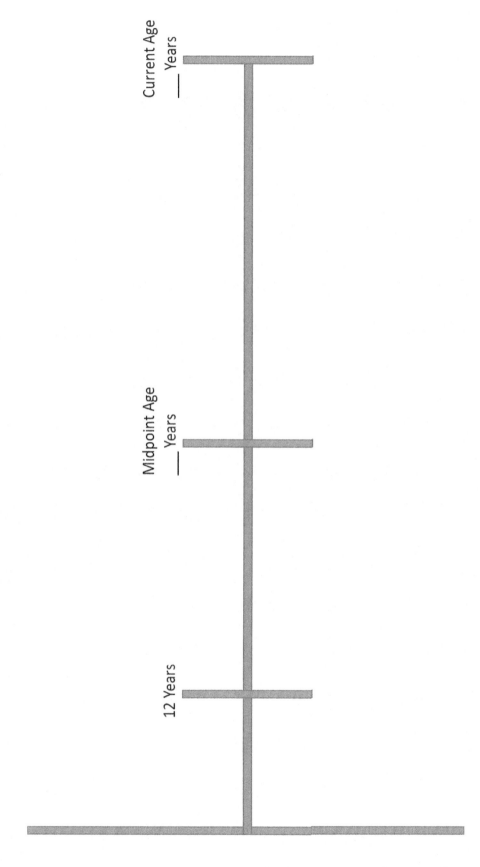

The Stickman: A Model of Belief Formation

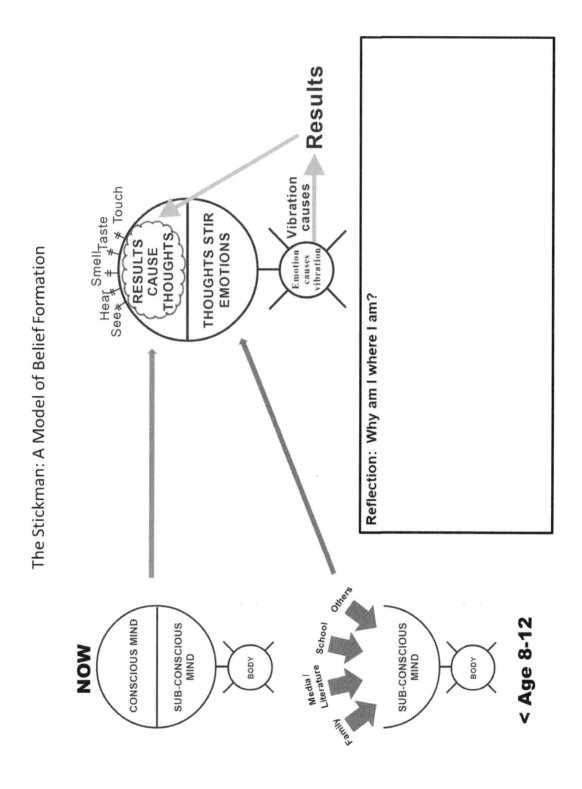

My Image Worksheet

My Top 3 Values:

1. _____   2. _____   3. _____

If you could see yourself 2 years from now, what and who would you like to see? Write it inside the mirror below:

The Image I Desire

No Matter What: HOLD YOUR IMAGE!

Made in the USA
Middletown, DE
06 June 2021